How to Avoid Catching....

The "Bridezilla" Virus

(Clipped Version)

A Practical (and Humorous) Shortened Guide to Managing & Avoiding Wedding Stress

By

Karen Korene

Throughout her art career, Karen Korene has dominated the floral industry specializing in wedding and special event design. Korene is an innovated, creative person whose witty personality enlightens audiences with her unique visions. As one of the youngest women inducted into the American Institute of Floral Designers (AIFD), Korene has won numerous local and national floral design competitions including the 1986 Dow Chemical design competition, 1996 FTD's America's Cup in which Korene was given the most prestigious honor of representing the United States in the 1997 Interfloral World Cup floral design competition. Her passion for flowers and love of weddings established Korene to become a creative force in the wedding industry. An accomplished writer, floral designer, wedding specialist, and photographer, Korene's busy schedule still allows her time to stop, smell, and photograph the roses.

The Bridezilla Virus ©2017 by Karen Korene

www.thebridezillavirus.com

ISBN-13: 978-1729564318
ISBN-10: 1729564313

Printed in the U.S.A.

Prologue

As a child I grew up reading fairytales. Like most young girls, I wanted to be Cinderella, living in a castle, and married to my handsome Prince. Our wedding would be a grand event suitable for royalty. With a Horse drawn carriage, lavish flowers, a beautiful ball-gown, and glass slippers, I was a princess and the center of attention.

As a teenager, I continued to dream of my fairy tale wedding and started to develop specific details of "my" special day. I purchased bridal magazines and spent hours tearing out pictures of wedding dresses, accessories, decorations, and flowers. I purchased an expandable file folder from a local office supply store and began a storage filing system of ideas for my dream wedding. In time, I had everything I ever wanted for my wedding day except for the groom.

As I approached a marrying age, my expandable file folder nearly reached its capacity. Several more file folders were added to handle the overflow of ideas. Throughout the years, my wedding ideas changed and matured. With the birth of the internet my expandable file folders were replaced with digital files. The grandeur of my wedding continued to grow. With numerous wedding ideas at my fingertips, I pinned, clicked, and downloaded wedding ideas fit for a princess. I just needed the ring to put my plans into motion.

When your Prince Charming or significant other enters your life and the big moment of an engagement arrives, all the childhood dreams of your fairytale wedding will emerge. As you begin to plan your wedding, the royal nightmare begins. When reality comes into play and the dream wedding is not obtainable, the bride may be infected with "wedding-perfection-itis" or what I call the "Bridezilla Virus."

"B" is for...

"Wedding-perfection-itis" or better known as the bridezilla virus is a disease which causes a transformation to begin within the bride who wants her wedding to be perfect.

Bridezilla symptoms:

- Stubborn
- Unrealistic
- Unwilling to accept substitutions or change
- Demanding
- Difficult to rationalize
- Obnoxious
- Self- centered
- Angry
- Micro manager
- Alienate friends, family, significant other.
- Mean
- Rude

Are weddings all about the bride?

- A wedding celebration traditionally focuses on the bride, but a wedding is for the groom, the parents, the grandparents, your siblings, friends, and various other individuals I failed to mention.
- Most often the planning process is left to the bride or brides' family.

Get Vaccinated

- Go on a "wedding date" with your fiancé.
- Take a Wedding Quiz (available at www.thebridezillavirus.com)

A few of the questions to ask and answer about your wedding are:
- What day would like to get married?
- Where would you like to be married?
- What type of wedding would you like to have?
- What time of day would you like the ceremony to be performed?
- How many guests would you like to attend?
- How much can we afford to spend on a wedding?
- How many attendants would you like stand up?
- What type of food would you like to serve?
- What colors or theme would you like to have?
- What type of entertainment?

List everything you **<u>disliked</u>** about going to weddings and avoid these items.

Top guest complaints:
- Inconvenient wedding date
- Not knowing where to go/ no map or directions
- Waiting for the ceremony to begin
- Not enough seating for ceremony
- Too much time between ceremony and reception
- Too large of distance from ceremony to reception
- No seating chart/ seated with strangers
- Long speeches
- Bad dining experience- cold or lack of food
- No knowledge of a Cash bar or poor bar service
- Music too loud / Inappropriate music type
- Room temperature- too hot or too cold
- Cramped spaces or too spacious
- Centerpieces obstructing views
- Ungracious hosts
- Disorganization and lulls
- Left without a ride for out of town guests
- Badly behaved bridal party

The Three C's of Wedding Planning

1. Communication
2. Cooperation
3. Consideration

Our marriage...Their wedding!

- Family and friends love to voice their opinions, views, and wants.
- Schedule another "wedding" date with your fiancé.
- Discuss the proposed changes, the monetary requirements, and possible solutions.
- A little schmoozing goes a long way to avoid hurt feelings.

Contests, Drawings, and Expo's ...oh my!

Wedding shows can be a wedding planning overload to your senses.

To achieve a successful wedding show outing:
- **Create a special email address** only for wedding information
- **Bring labels** with your name, address, phone, wedding date, and email address for prize drawings.
- **Wear comfortable shoes.**
- **Wear comfortable clothing.**
- **Bring friends, family, or bridal party** with you to share in the experience
- **Make a plan.** Make of list of what you are shopping for. It should ease any anxiety from wedding planning overload.

Go the show/expo hungry. Forget the diet…. eat, drink, and have fun!

#getting married

Create a wedding website and include the following:
- Story of the proposal
- Story of your relationship
- Date of the wedding
- Countdown clock (optional)
- Directions to wedding ceremony/reception for wedding guests
- Wedding party bio's
- Hotel information
- Transportation options for out of town guests
- Wedding timelines and updates
- Menu options- may also be a help for those with food allergies
- Gift Registry information
- Suggestion Board

To avoid the most popular mistakes of social media, a bride should avoid the following:
- Posting Incessantly
- Using social media on your wedding day.
- Losing it with hashtags.
- Going off on Facebook
- Getting too sappy
- Going radio silent.
- Letting people use social media during the ceremony.
- Continuous selfies

I don't think so!

- A disagreement or an argument is inevitable with most people.
- Inoculate with knowledge, conquer with organization and eliminate with communication.
- Your fiancé may not be helping with the wedding is **NOT** a sign that they do not care.
- Parents may feel it is a reflection of them.
- Try not to become self-absorbed with wedding planning.
- Be open to criticism, humbled by complements, and thankful you have friends in your life that stand by your side to witness and celebrate your marriage.
- Respect your vendors and listen to their advice, they are the professionals.

Not quite what I would pick

- Invited guests, friends, and family will have certain expectations when attending your wedding

- People judge others often because they are comparing themselves to another person.

- Don't get discouraged or hurt feelings....it are not their wedding, it's yours!

Budget or busted?

Determine the total amount you have to spend on the wedding celebration.

Use the bullet points below to give an approximate amount you can spend on each item.

- Venue – from 5% - 13%
    - Including facility fees for both ceremony/reception
    - Marriage Officiate fee, wedding license fee, transportation fee
- Food / Beverage – from 30% - 64%
    - Including appetizers, dinner, cake, candy/ sweet table, beverages (alcohol /non-alcoholic selections)
- Photography / Video – from 10% - 16%
- Including photographer's fees, proofs, flash drives, wedding albums
    - Entertainment – from 5% - 15%
        - Including ceremony, dinner, and reception entertainment (band, DJ, photo booth, etc.)
    - Rentals – from 3% - 17%
        - Including chairs, tables, linens
    - Flowers / Decorations – from 6% - 12%
        - Including ceremony, reception, and personal flowers
        - Candles, vases, wedding favors, invitation, postage
    - Bridal beauty
    - Gifts/gratuities.

Do not go in debt planning/hosting a wedding.

Staying organized

1. **Write everything down.**
2. **Consider a color coding system.**
3. **Communicate clearly**
4. **Start early.**
5. **Plan to plan**
6. **Store all of your wedding items in one place.**
7. **Color code once again**

Do I know you???

- Follow the basic rule of thirds….your family, your fiancé's family, and the wedding couple.
- Use the concept of the "police lineup"…. if you could recognize them in a police lineup, do not invite them.
- Divide the total wedding cost per number of guests to determine the cost of each guest to be invited IF you need get budget in line with relatives wanting to go over allotted guest number.

Paper trail

The typical invitation includes:

- The invitation with two envelopes (outer and inner)
- The reception card
- The response card
- The response card envelope (which requires postage)
- Additional pages and cards that provide directions, hotel information, even gift registry information.

To avoid costly mistakes, keep in mind the following:

- The number of invitations does not equal the number of guests. Married couples and families receive one invitation
- Knowing the invitation count gives you the total number of thank you cards, RSVP cards, and wedding stationery needed.
- Cost per invitation will vary on the quantity and quality of materials used.
- Enclosures that are added will increase the cost of postage by added weight to the envelope
- Addressing services will add to the cost but will save you hours of tedious inscription.
- Postage is not limited to the outer envelope; response cards must have postage.
- Hidden costs will always be present. Here are a few "hidden" costs that may occur:

  - Special Ink (for the DIY invites)

  - Proofs – a proof is necessary to avoid misspelled words, incorrect addresses, and wrong times.

  - Custom colors, special fonts, special paper will increase the cost

  - Odd-shaped envelopes & unique fasteners add bulk and weight to the invitation; it may also add a special handling fee by the post office.

- Purchase a few extra invitations and envelopes to allow for errors.

Dress + Diet = Disaster

Look in the mirror…this is the person your fiancé fell in love with.

Entering into a life change should be done for personal health reasons and not to fit into a wedding dress.

- Choose who will accompany the bride (better known as the "support team") to bridal dress shopping.
- Plan a dress shopping meeting, party, or girl's night.
- Make a shopping plan

To avoid dress drama:

- Make your dress appointment early in the day when sale associates are fresh and cheerful.
- Try not to eat or drink before your appointment. Being bloated does not help with self-esteem.
- Wear undergarments that make you feel pretty, sexy, and special. No need for special shoes at this time.
- Bring a camera and have a member of your support team take pictures of you in each dress you try on. This is a wonderful way to see how you look in each dress and in photos. What we envision and what the camera sees are totally different. In addition, it is a great way to remember the day.
- When considering gown styles keep in mind the style of your venue. A ball gown may be out of place on a beach.
- Trust your instincts – you will know when to say "yes" to a dress.

DON'T LOOK AT THE DRESS SIZE….ORDER A SIZE THAT FITS WELL!

Let's get physical!

- Check with your health care professional to avoid any future health issues.
- Consult a professional fitness specialist to instruct you how to properly tone the targeted areas
- Enhance the areas that are exposed such as your arms, shoulders, back, neck, etc. IF unable to do an entire body workout.

Wrestling your underwire

- Proper foundation is the most important part of the wedding attire.
- Consult a professional to fit and suggest the proper undergarments needed to make your wedding gown fit like a glove
- Choose of bathroom accessibility undergarments
- Test your undergarments for an entire day to see if you need to replace any uncomfortable items.
- Bring the necessary foundation items to your dress alteration

The Glass Slipper Syndrome

Consider the following:

- Will these shoes be seen?
- If your shoes are not being seen go for comfort and a second pair for style.
- Are they comfortable when I first put them on?
- Is the fabric stretchable to allow for your feet to swell?
- Are your toes able to move or are they cramped together?

- Are you able to walk easily on all surfaces without assistance?
- Is there any type of support in the shoe to allow you to wear this shoe for an extended period of time?
- Does this shoe stay on while walking or dancing?

Create a chart of "shoe" timeline.

- Possibly start with flats/slippers before the ceremony
- Stylish heels for the actual ceremony
- Walking shoes for photos
- Reception and dancing shoes
- Finish with your original flats/slippers

If a foot massage is not available, use a tennis ball!

It's Sew Perfect... or is it?

An emergency sewing kit should have the following:
- Large safety pins for a broken bustle
- Zipper ease or white crayon for a stuck zipper
- Tide to Go Pen or Shout Wipes for miscellaneous stains
- White chalk to cover miscellaneous stains
- Double sided tape to fix fallen hem
- Clean white terry-cloth towel to brush dirt away from bottom of dress
- Travel size garment steamer
- Q-tips
- Needle and thread
- Scissors
- Clear nail polish

Gossip Girls

Have a meet and greet girl's night
- Discuss your wedding ideas, dress color, style, and monetary expectations.
- We are all different but share a common interest…. the wedding.

The Leader of the Pack

The maid of honor becomes a therapist, go-for and go-to person, time keeper, fashion expert, party planner (bridal shower, bachelorette,) rule enforcer, and liaison between the bride and bridesmaids.

The MOH-zilla generally sees her position as maid of honor as a sign of power over the other bridesmaids.

Mini Me

Children are unpredictable and not always controllable.
Most children:
- Are on a schedule.
- Eat at a certain time
- Eat certain foods
- Takes scheduled nap
- Have play time
- Go to bed at a designated hour

Any deviation from the above items and it becomes possible for unfavorable behavior
- To place a child in a stressful, chaotic situation with strangers, unfamiliar surroundings, uncomfortable clothing, and several hundred eyes watching their every move; a child is bound to act differently.

- Most disruptive behavior occurs when a child is not watched or allowed to do things that normally would be denied.
- Something will go wrong with a child in the wedding party, accept the outcome without blame.

"Ruff" Time

- See if your venue will allow pets (other than service animals) on the property.

- Prepare them for the big day. This includes multiple trial runs at the venue, crowd conditioning, and additional obedience classes.

- Most pets do not feel comfortable wearing clothing.

- Pets are a challenge for your photographer.

- Inform your guests with allergies that a pet may be present at the celebration.

- A wedding is a stressful environment and your pet may not like or want the attention.

- If you are stressed, they will be stressed and act out for attention.

- Think of what is best for your pet (and for you) on your wedding day.

My Signature Colors are...

The color(s) of your wedding sets the mood of the celebration before you choose a color pallet:

- Consider your venue
  - The venue will certainly play a key role with wedding colors. Trying to cover up or distract from the venue colors to coordinate with the wedding colors is a costly endeavor.
- The time of year
  - Just like your wardrobe, the season can influence your wedding color palette. Pastels look better in spring while dark tones are better suited for fall. There are no exact "rules" for this but it will be easier to find items in the given season rather than out of season.
- Set the mood
  - Color sets the mood for a wedding as much as time of day, location, or time of year. If you prefer a more dramatic look, then the dark rich jewel tones would work better than pastels.

Matchy - Matchy

- If there is no variance in color everything will appear dull & undistinguishable.

<u>*Nothing* will ever be the same color.</u>

<u>Sliding Scale</u>

Ask yourself before deciding on decorating your venue(s) are:
- How long will we be using the venue space?
- How large is the venue space?
  - Room size
  - Ceiling height
    - Notice if there are hanging lights, beams, or chandeliers
  - Flooring type
  - Table size

A typical place setting is approximately 18" wide and 15" deep (table edge to center of table.)

- 72" round table (seats 8-10) – 24" available space
- 60" round table (seats 6-8) – 20" available space
- 48" round table (seats 4-6) – 18" available space
- 6' / 8' long tables (tables are 30" wide) – no available space without invading the place setting

<u>ALWAYS</u> ask the venue before installing any decorations.

<u>NEVER</u> assume you are able to use nails, tape or glue in the venue without written consent.

<u>Don't Get Poked</u>

- Pinterest offers a couple hundreds, if not thousands of wedding ideas.
- May have unreasonable expectations for their wedding from pins.
- Unable to grasp the fact that not everyone is able to create the items posted on Pinterest.
- To the budget conscious bride with limited time and finances, the outcome of the attempted craft or project may not be as shown, take ten times the amount of time to construct, and costs more than purchasing the same item off Etsy or having a professional create it.
- Try to replicate the pins but take bits and pieces of favored pins and incorporate them into your celebration at the level of crafting ability at hand.
- Create one main public board for discussion of ideas.
- Create one main private board to avoid criticism from others.
- Pin everything at first and then streamline your picks.
- Stop pinning when decisions are made and orders placed with vendors.

Remember.... Pinterest = Inspiration

<u>DIY......LMAO!</u>

Do it yourself (DIY) projects are a wonderful money saver and a way for the bride, her mother, friends, and other family members to showcase their talents

A few things to consider when considering a DIY project are:
- The finished product rarely looks like the picture.
- Additional materials may be needed to enhance the finished product
- Frustration sets in when the final result is not what you envisioned
- Extraordinary time commitment to complete the projects
- One is doable, ten is bearable, thirty is insanity, and three hundred is just plain nuts.
- Storage requirements for finished projects
- Transportation and set up of finished projects
- Removal of finished projects
- Disposal of finished projects
- Finished products may cost more than purchasing them already finished
- If it is a time-sensitive project or too large of a project to take on then do not risk it.

Five main items that should be left to professionals:
1. Flowers
2. Your Hair
3. Planning/Coordination
4. Photography
5. Food

If you do not procrastinate, then a diy project is a wonderful way of putting a personal touch to your wedding celebration.

Blooming Miracles

Special considerations should be made when purchasing fresh flowers.

Keep in mind the following:
- Type of flowers
  - Certain flowers have a strong fragrance that could trigger allergies. Swollen itchy eyes, runny nose, sinus pressure, headaches and a sore throat are not wanted symptoms for your wedding day.
- Seasonal availability
  - Certain flowers are only available during specific seasons. Limited availability may be available from Holland, South America, or California but they come at a cost.
- Perishable
  - Fresh flowers are perishable and not meant to live forever.

Wedding flowers are divided into three main categories
- Personal
  - Any flower(s) presented to a person to carry, wear, or toss
- Ceremony
  - Any flower(s) or plants used to enhance the ceremony location, and aisle decoration.
- Reception
  - Include table centerpieces, head table decoration, guest book adornment, place card & gift table flowers, cake top, and cake table flowers.

Bridal bouquet basics:
- The style of bouquet should complement and not detract from the wedding gown and the bride
- The larger the bouquet, the heavier the bouquet is to carry

Piece of Cake

Cake shopping is not for the faint of heart. It requires a base layer of food to absorb the sugar, something to cleanse the pallet between varieties, and of course…. stretchy pants!

Before you dive in and make appointments:
- Have a guest count to determine size of cake needed
- Bring examples of wedding cake styles you prefer
- Make a list of cake flavors you are interested in
- Bring examples of wedding cake decoration ideas
- Bring any accessories you would like incorporated with the cake
- Be open to suggestions and let your baker mix up some magic!

Order a piece of cake for each guest attending the wedding

If the wedding cake is being served, the wait staff will serve a piece of cake to each place setting even if no one is present.

Caterers will panic if there is not enough cake to go around so please avoid having the bridezilla virus affect your caterer and wait staff, order enough cake.

Freeze Frame

- A picture is worth a lifetime of memories and preserves the celebration documentation for generations.
- Wedding photos document history, capture trends, and comic poses of drunken family and friends.
- You are hiring a photographer's creative expression, talent, knowledge, and personality.

Your photographer will show you everything you may have missed. If anyone has any tension on the wedding day it will show in the wedding pictures

- On your wedding day do not try to act like a supermodel.
- Un-natural poses may be awkward and unflattering.
- Do not have unrealistic expectations; trust your photographer to bring you best side forward.
- Don't over tan… an un-natural orange glow from a bottle or tanning bed may make you look like an alien from your favorite movie.
- Photoshop can help some pictures but it is a costly process.

- Make sure your camera phone enthusiasts do not get in the way of your photographer
- Ask family members and friends to "just get along" for the photos.

Musical Chairs

Seating chart will:

- Avoid confusion on where to sit
- Avoid potential guest seating issues
- Eliminate unfilled tables
- Enhance the overall guest experience
- Deters uninvited guests to "pop" in for a free meal
- Informs you who did not show up for the celebration

To avoid seating issues

- Get a basic seating chart of proposed floor plan from venue
- Use a seating chart apps or free websites to make the seating chart process much easier
- Start a seating chart once the RSVP's arrive and immediately begin assigning guests to tables.
- Do not seat some of the parents at the bridal table unless you can seat all-including stepparents
- Do assign guests to table where they know someone
- Do not seat all of your guests with only people they've met before.
- Do not play matchmaker with your single guests.
- Do consider your guest's personalities and interests while assigning tables.

Plus, one?

- Do not give in to pressure from guests to allow an additional person
- Personal call rather than waiting for an email that may not be seen or answered
- Be firm but understanding yet gracious and thank them for understanding.

When children are included on the RVSP and it is an adult only affair....

- Allow only one person to deal with the "children" issue.
- Be sure to explicitly state in your invitations your views on having children being present or not being present at your event. Your guests may try to find a loop hole to squeeze their children into attending.
- Be aware that if a guest threatens not to come, the rudeness is theirs and not yours.

Mama-saurus...WRECKS!

Mothers become infected by "wedding-perfection-itis" and turns into a Mama-saurus who can wreck your wedding. Several variations or types of the Mama-saurus:

- the vicarious
- the critical
- the emotional
- the angry
- the controlling

Signs your mother is turning or has turned into a controlling mama-saurus are:

- **Makes you doubt yourself**
  - Since childhood she makes you feel like you are a child. Nothing you do will ever be right. Decisions you make are wrong if you did not consult her.
- **Psychotic stalking**
  - She needs to know where you are at all times. She is nosy and will cyber stalk you.
- **Controlling relationships and friends**
  - She will dominate conversations and eaves drop on others conversations to dominate them as well.
- **Guilt trips you**
  - She will whine on how little time you are spending with her and then talk in a small, weak, worn voice to show how she is suffering. If you stand your ground she will send you multiple text messages, emails, or phone calls with words to make you feel guilty for having an opinion.

- **Lies, belittles, condemning, and abuses you**
  - She is a proficient liar and mastered how to rally others to believe her web of deceit. Anyone who gives her an audience will receive an Oscar winning performance. She will always have a scowl on her face and manages to isolate you from your friends. She is first to point out your weaknesses and will embarrass you every chance she gets.
- **Gives you gifts with strings-attached**
  - She will graciously give you a gift and then use this gesture to make you do things for her. She will bring up things she has done for you and make you feel obligated to return the favor.

- **Competes for yours and everyone's attention**
  - She will drive your friends away so you are solely dependent on her. It is a form of isolation that puts her above everything else in your life.

In the mind of Mama-saurus she will believe that if you take her advice, allow or accept a change she implicated, it now gives her free reign to alter your wedding plans to her liking.

- Get back control of your wedding and your life without causing your mother pain and anguish

- Understand that your mother/mother in law has emotions, feelings, and dreams about the milestones in your life including your wedding. Feelings of anxiety and abandonment may appear in your mother/mother in law

- Be firm in your wedding vision but do make your mother/mother in law feel included in your day.

Make a list of the no-compromise details. If they are paying for the wedding it does not give them the right to change anything without your approval. You may have to graciously decline a monetary gift and pay for your wedding cerebration yourself

Give your mom a task that isn't as important to you to such as a bridesmaid's luncheon, farewell brunch, welcome bag construction, or gift opening to plan.

It is NOT Mother's Day ….it's my wedding!

- Different from being a mama-sauraus, your mom begins to feel it is her day and she is in charge.

- Bad behavior from your mother may be her way of coping with the changes in her life.

- Use a diversion with reverse psychology

- On your wedding day do something special for your mom. Give her a letter thanking her helping you become the person you are today.

- Remind her you need her for advice and help when solicited since marriage can be challenging.

- You may want to present her with a small gift as a reminder how much she means to you.

"Weather" it's nice or not

- You cannot control the weather!

- Have an alternate plan or plans in place with a separate person in charge to implement a change or changes if necessary.

- Embrace the positives of the situations and move on to plan B, C, etc.

It's my wedding… (And I will cry if I want to)

- A rollercoaster of emotions surface planning a wedding

- Meltdowns appear when the bride feels misunderstood and alone.

- Meltdowns take various forms and range in intensity.

Use any of all of the following to get through your meltdown.

- **Cry** – A good cry is a wonderful physiological stress relieving option. Crying is not a sign of weakness but it feels good to get it all out.
- **Walk away** – When you are unable to be rational in your thinking or actions it is best to walk away, calm down, and gain clarity of the situation.
- **Find the root of the problem** – Finding the root of the problem will eliminate future outbreaks.
- **Don't procrastinate** - Deal with issues as soon as you can.
- **Don't hold on to problems that have been fixed.**

Whatever is bothering you let it go to gain control back in your life.

It's not what I thought it would feel like.

- No two people are the same and everyone will have their own experience.
- It is best not to listen to anyone telling you how to feel. Trust in yourself and be present for the moment.
- The love in your heart for the person you are committing yourself to is the one main emotion you should focus on.

You're backing out??

If a vendor cancels an event, it means you have been affected by the bridezilla virus.

Vendors do not cancel an event unless they feel it is unlikely for them to perform the service you requested.

- Unable to make a decision
- Changing you mind on a continuous basis
- Adding to your order and not accepting the added cost
- Too many emails, phone calls, or instant messages over non-relative issues
- Wedding couple being demanding
- Family members (mostly mothers) being demanding
- Unrealistic expectations
- Unfavorable reviews
- Lack of respect and/or manners

No vendor wants to lose business but sometimes it is necessary to avoid future conflict, negative reviews, or failure to receive payment on services rendered.

What If….

- Two simple words that when put together can cause fear for any person
- Obsessing over one or any "what if" situations can cause the bridezilla virus to emerge, grow, and flourish.
- Stop saying "what if" and accept "what is
- Stop worrying about little missed details and be present on the day

Sticker Shock

Once the bills are totaled, the deposits or retainers are deducted, and the remaining balance is more than you ever imagined…you are experiencing sticker shock.

- There is always something to add to a wedding celebration.
- A small change may seem innocent enough and affordable until the numbers are tallied.
- Think twice before adding anything… ask if it is a want or a need.
- Communicate honestly to your vendors and each other.
- Best to examine your wedding additions, the over budget amount, and signed contracts to see how to proceed to get your budget back under control.

Shooting yourself with bullet points!

- Lists upon lists with bullet points will appear on post-it notes in random places.
- Brides begin to get overwhelmed causing most to be a bit scatterbrained.
- Condense the wedding planner; trust in your vendors, and start prepping with your day of coordinator at least 4 weeks prior to the event.

- Do create a mini version of your wedding plan. Include the key people, contact phone numbers (with alternate phone numbers too,) delivery times, and any remarks of that vendor.

Don't let the bridezilla virus ruin your event; Delegate, eliminate, and articulate.

"Bin" there

Storage totes or bins are available in various sizes. . I suggest purchasing plastic ones with an attached hinged cover if possible. Plastic bins are reusable, most often water-proof, and stackable.

- Have large bins available for each bridesmaid, mothers, and yourself. Label each bin with each name and advise everyone that it is for ALL of their personal items. The pre wedding staging area will stay clutter free and there is a lesser chance of items getting lost or stolen. The bins can then be transferred to the reception location while the bridal party is off taking photos and celebrating the marriage.

- Keep packing material together for each item brought to the ceremony and reception. Separate boxes that are clearly marked with the items in the box will allow the clean-up crew to keep items organized and easily transportable.

- Create a master list of the bins along with who will be in charge of set-up and breakdown. A numbering system works well.

- Keep a separate smaller bin with items that can be reached easily to help the bride throughout the day. Items such as: several pair of shoes, breath mints, aspirin, medication, deodorant, tennis ball (for a fast foot massage), feminine hygiene products, etc.

- Have an emergency kit available for life's little mishaps.

- Bins should also be purchased to pack your wedding gifts for transport home.

Purchase a folding cart. This ($50-$70) investment is a life and time saver.

What was that?

Bridal brain (also known as BB) is the temporary condition of forgetfulness and the silent celebration killer.

Several areas where bridal brain prevails in the early stages of wedding planning are:

- Not setting up in-person appointments.
- Not asking for referrals.
- Not reading the fine print
- Not requesting samples
- Not keeping a paper trail
- Not keeping up with your wedding website

Several last minute items that are often forgotten are:
- **Thank you gifts**
  - A thank you gift is customary for the bridal party as a sign of appreciation
  - Favors for the wedding guests
  - Groom's gift
  - Parent's gift
- **Wrapping gifts**
- **Vendor meals**
  - It is necessary to feed your vendors (band members, DJ, photographer, videographer, any assistants)
- **Marriage license**

On your wedding day,

- **Eat/ Hydrate**
- **Use the rest room**
- **Put on a button-down shirt**

After the vows have been said, rings exchanged, and you are married

- Take several minutes with your partner to treasure the moment. Steal a kiss, hold each other, and be in the moment. This may be the only chance you get to be alone all day.
- Put your marriage license in a safe place.

You need it? I got it!!

Create several individual kits- bride, bridesmaids, groom, parents, and guests. A parts organizer box (available from your local hardware or box store)

Some items to include in your kits are:
- Alcohol (if all else fails)
- Baby powder
- Blotting papers
- Breath mints or mouth wash
- Bug spray
- Cash
- Cell phone
- Cell phone charger
- Chap stick
- Cooling towel
- Curling iron/flat iron
- Dental floss
- Dental floss/toothpicks

- Deodorant
- Extension cord
- Extra earring backs
- Eye drops
- Feminine products
- Flash light/matches
- Hair brush/comb
- Hair clips, bobby pins
- Hair spray/ hair gel
- Hand lotion
- Hand sanitizer
- Iron, steamer, or wrinkle remover
- Lighter
- Lint roller
- Make up- powder, blush, lip stick, cover up etc.
- Medicine (pain reliever, allergy, antacid)
- Mini first aid kit (band-aids, burn-relief, antiseptic gel)
- Mini sewing kit with scissors, needles, thread, buttons, and safety pins.
- Nail clipper
- Nail file
- Nail polish (clear and color you are wearing)
- Pen/ paper
- Phone numbers of all wedding participants
- Q-tips @ makeup remover
- Razor
- Saline solution
- Snacks-granola bar, protein bar
- Stain remover pen
- Static cling spray
- Straws
- Sunscreen
- Super Glue
- Tennis ball
- Tissues
- Tooth brush/tooth paste

- Towel-ettes or baby wipes
- Tweezers
- Umbrella
- Utility knife
- Water
- White chalk
- White duct tape or hem tape

Attitude with a Twist...

Body language is the nonverbal expression of your feelings
- Crossed arms and legs signal resistance to your ideas.
- Real smiles crinkle the eyes.
- Copying others body language.
- Posture
- Eyes that lie
- Raised eyebrows
- Exaggerated nodding signals anxiety about approval
- A clenched jaw signals stress

Takeover/Timing Tyrants

Friends and family will remind you of your timeline and schedule constantly during the wedding day
- Do not over book your time
- Expect everything to take longer than planned on the wedding day.
- Allow extra time for traffic while traveling.
- Be prepared that something will go wrong or not as planned.

With proper organization, proper communication, and acceptance of what "is" and not what it should be, your day will be imperfect as expected.

Takeover tyrants appear in various forms- be your future in-laws, a picky bridesmaid, a know-it-all wedding guest, or even an overeager wedding guest with the best intentions.

When a takeover tyrant assumes a non-appointed position in your wedding it is best for the day of wedding coordinator to intercede on your behalf.

If they insist on helping you some small task for them to complete such as greeting guests, assisting those guests with special needs or aiding with breakdown or distribution/dismantling of wedding decorations.

Lights, Camera, Action!

The mood is very relaxed until you put on your wedding dress. Suddenly you realize that you have become the center of attention.

- To avoid anxiety, it is best to withdraw into a bubble walking down the aisle
- A stress relieving tactic is to lean on those who will accompany you down the aisle for support.
- Don't hide behind your bridal bouquet
    - Practice with your bouquet before the ceremony it will save you years of regret from photographs

Keep your vows to the point, sincere, and speak from the heart.
    - Don't go into a production or expect one.
    - Swelling fingers is not uncommon to occur during the wedding ceremony. If the ring does not readily go on, do not force it!

Stealing the Spotlight

Someone may try to steal your spotlight and turn your day into their own.
- Confront them right away.
- Put a humorous spin on the event.
- Take the edge off the incident and joke about it.
- Immediately turn the focus back to the main event…the wedding.
- Your first instinct will be one of defense and anger. Step back, breathe, and remember if you let it bother you….it will.

You Ruined MY Wedding!

Something, someone, or even your significant other's actions may trigger you to be upset, angry, envious, or even irate.

Some of the actions of others that may push you over the edge are:
- Hung over bridal party from the rehearsal dinner or bachelor party
- Showing up with a date who wasn't invited or liked
- Showing up late
- Incessantly texting or taking photos during the ceremony
- Speaking up during the ceremony
- Sticking a finger in the wedding cake
- Someone wearing white (or ivory) other than the bride
- Giving a "roast" rather than a toast
- Using your wedding to hook up at the event itself
- Drinking too much – it's a wedding celebration, not a fraternity party!
- Spilling anything on the bride
- Letting the kids run wild
- Telling the DJ to change the music
- Playing a joke on the bridal party

- Destroying property of the venue, wedding couple, or guests
- Having the police called to break up a fight
- Telling the bride, she could have looked better on her wedding day

Worry about confronting anyone about any mishaps until after the wedding has ended.

Is it over yet?

- Wedding planning is an emotional rollercoaster that a couple rides not only for the duration of the wedding planning, but on the wedding day and through life.

- Even with your best laid plans, there will be multiple questions for the couple on their wedding day.

- An annoyed state of mind does not give you the right to be rude, insensitive, or mean.

- The wedding experience is mentally and physically exhausting.

- A wedding is not about the celebration; it is about the commitment between the two of you.

Now What?

Your wedding celebration is never truly over.
Begin the following tasks as soon as possible after the wedding:

- Thank you notes
    - Good etiquette is to have thank you notes mailed within 90 days of the wedding.
- Cleaning your wedding dress
    - Fresh stains are easier to clean than ones that have been sitting for a while.

- Toss/dispose of any wedding items not worth saving
  - Keep your favorite mementoes and dispose of the rest.
- Insuring your wedding rings
  - A lost ring is heartbreaking. Make it less painful with a replacement policy.
- Request copies of your marriage license
  - Have several copies available for any name change forms, insurance, or where proof of marriage is necessary

Take it slow…don't rush into your next big project…house, baby, etc. Always be prepared and remember to use the three "C's" in life, they will never let you down. Failing to do so may lead you to becoming a "B" and it will not mean bridezilla!

References

A bride has so many sources to plan her wedding. In previous years, the majority of bridal ideas were found in the library, bookstore, or magazine. Now ideas, trends, and projects are at your fingertips just a click away.

Several amazing articles and websites were used to gather information for this book. I encourage you to visit these websites and read the articles for additional information.

Anton, Carrie. "*11 Mistakes Couples Make That Drive Photographers Crazy (in GIFs)*. The Knot. Web. 15 May 2017.

"Are Weddings all about the Bride?." *Weddingpartyapp.com.* Blog. May 2016.

Bolt, Ken. "Wedding Flowers-the Origins of the Tradition." *Feelingsandflowers.com.* 01 February 2008. Web. September 2016.

Bender, Michelle. "*Beat the Post-Wedding Blues.*" Bridal Guide. Web. 07 July 2017.

"Bouquet Etiquette-How to hold your bouquet." *The Knot.* Web. June 2017.

Bradberry, Travis. "*8 Great Tricks for Reading People's Body Language.*" 18 May 2016. www.entrepreneur.com. Web. 15 July 2017.

Brideandgroom.com. Web. May 2016.

"Brides' Biggest Wedding Day Fears." *The Knot.* Web. October 2016.

Brockway, Rev. Laurie Sue. "Signs You are Too Stressed About Your Wedding." *huffingtonpost.com.* 07 April 2016. Web. June 2016.

Clayton, Elizabeth. "Wedding Seating Chart: Everything You Need To Know." *A Practical Wedding.* Practical Media Inc. 2009. Web. 12 Oct. 2016.

Dainton, Lottie."*7 Things to consider when involving your pet at your wedding.*" weddingideasmag, Web, 30 June 2015.

Diproperio, Linda. "6 Last Minute Details Brides Always Forget." SHEfinds. 19 April 2017. Web. May 2017.

Diproperio, Linda. "6 Things Brides Forget To Do When Getting Ready For The Big Day." SHEfinds. 29 May 2017. Web. May 2017.

Diproperio, Linda. "6 Things Brides Forget When Planning Their Wedding Online." SHEfinds. 16 May 2017. Web. May 2017.

Durand Streisand, Elizabeth. "12 Surprising Reasons Why Your Feet Hurt." 23 October 2015. *GoodHousekeeping.com.* July 2016.

Eckert, Tammy. "When Brides Attack – 5 Tips for Dealing With a Bridezilla." *Huffingtonpost.com.* 06 May 2016. Web. June 2016.

"Establishing your Budget." *The Knot.* Web. December 2015.

Gatulis, Rachel. "What to do when the wedding planning meltdown begins." *Baltimoresun.com.* 15 November 2012. Web. August 2016.

Gonzalez, Xochitl. "5 Biggest Wedding Day Fears: How to Get Over Them." *Weddings.about.com.* Web. October 2016.

Guth, Tracy. "How to Seat Your Wedding Reception Guests." *The Knot.*
	Web. October 2016.
Herring, Amber. "8 Signs You've Become a Bridezilla." 29 January 2015.
	Womenshealthmag.com. Web. February 2016.
Hill, Simone. "8 Steps to Choosing Your Wedding Colors." *The Knot.* Web.
	October 2016.
"How To Create a Wedding Website that Wows Your Guests." 21 May
	2016. *Design Inspiration.* Wix Blog.
"How to Deal with Wedding Guest Who Try to Add an Uninvited Plus-
	One." *Huffingtonpost.com.* 29 May 2014. Web. June 2017.
"How to Tame a Momzilla without Offending Her." *Brides.* 18 July 2014.
	Web June 2016.
Jeanish. "Biggest Seating Chart Mistakes." *ProjectWedding.com.* 24 May
	2014. Web. October 2016.
Kaforey, Karen. "Maximizing Your Wedding Budget." *Brideandgroom.com.*
	Web. December 2015.
Kidder Nicole. "A Superstitious Wedding." *weddingtraditions.about.com.*
	Web. August 2016.
Klein, Kristen. *"The 10 Biggest Post-Wedding Mistakes Newlyweds Make."*
	Bridal Guide. Web. 18 June 2017.
"Leave It to the Professionals: 5 Things a Bride Should Never DIY."
	Brides.com. 20 May 2014. Web. June 2016.
Malone, Sandy. "Don't Let Momzilla Ruin Your Wedding: Five Steps You
	Can Take to Do Damage Control in Advance." *Huffingtonpost.com.* 27
	August 2012. Web. June 2016.
Malone, Sandy. "Only You Can Let Bad Weather Ruin Your Wedding
	Day." *Huffingtonpost.com.* 05 March 2015. Web. August 2016.
Martin, Stacie. "Surviving the Dreaded Momzilla." *Huffingtonpost.com.* 10
	September 2013. Web. June 2016.
Ngo, Cathy. "The Ultimate High Heel Survival Guide." 19 April 2015.
	www.buzzfeed.com. Web. July 2016.
Obenschain, Chris. "10 Signs You're Turning into Bridezilla." 18 May 2010.
	HowStuffWorks.com. Web. February 2016.
Osgood, Bradley. Personal Interview. 11 July 2017.
	"The Complete Guide to Wedding Invitations." *Invitopia.com* Web. 7 July
	2017.
"Pets at Weddings." *Circle of Love: weddings & event by design.* Web. 20
	January 2017.
Pfeffer, Stephanie Emma. "How to Deal with Wedding Crashers." *The
	Knot.* Web. June 2017.
Posner, Joanna. "How to Handle a Momzilla While Planning Your
	Wedding." *Inside Weddings.* Web. June 2016.
"Rain for Good Luck on your Wedding Day." *Weddingbee.com.* June 2012.
	Web. August 2016.
Rosenberg, Dr. Steven. "When your Feet Hurt, Everything Hurts. Ouch!"
	17 November 2011. *Huffingtonpost.com.* Web. July 2016.
Sainato, Stefania. "Top 10 Wedding Guest Complaints." 14 April 2014.
	Huffingpost Weddings. Web. May 2016.

Schipani, Denise. "The Seven Deadly Bridal Sins." *Bridal Guide*. Web. May
	2016.

Schwartz, Justine. "6 Social Media Mistakes Brides Make – But Shouldn't."
	SHEfinds. 22 February 2017. Web. July 2017.

"Shoe Selection Tips Help Our Golden Triangle Brides Avoid Wedding
	Day Foot Pain." *SETX Weddings.com*. Web. July 2016.

Simpson, Megan. "How to cope with Stage Fright on Your Wedding Day."
	Insideweddings.com. Web. October 2016.

Smith, Daniel. "Wedding Costs" Where Does All the Money Go? *Bridal
	Guide*. Web. July 2016.

Tantum, Stephanie. "Follow these tips for handling a bridal meltdown."
	Citizensvoice.com. 06 May 2012. Web. August 2016.

"Telling it like it is, not like it was: Signs that your mama is too
	controlling." *Jaber3000.blogspot.com*. July 2012. Web. July 2016.

"The Guest List Tug of War." *Theplunge.com*. Web. September 2016.

"The History of Wedding Traditions." BridalWhimsy.com.

"The Wedding Budget." *BridalWhimsy.com*. Brideandgroom.com. Web.
	May 2016.

"This is What Happens to Your Feet When You Wear High
	Heels." *www.thescienceofeating.com*. 10 June 2015. Web. July 2016.

Torgerson, Rachel. *"How to Create a Wedding Communication Plan." The
	Knot*. Web. June 2016.

"Woes of Wedding Warriors." *Shoesnfeet.com*. Web. July 2016

"3 Brides on the Fights They Always Have with Their Grooms." *Brides.com*.
	08 August 2015. Web. August 2016.

"4 Ways to Manage Your Wedding-Planning Meltdowns." *Brides.com*. 15
	July 2015. Web. August 2016.

"5 People Who Will Try to Take Over Your Wedding Day." *The Knot*. Web.
	October 2016.

"5 Things That Stress Out Brides the Most and How to Deal." *Brides*. 07
	January 2015. Web. June 2016.

"5 Ways to Deal with a Momzilla." *Dreamwedding.com*. 05 October 2015.
	Web. June 2016.

"7 Reasons You Want Rain on Your Wedding Day (Seriously!)." *Brides*. 10
	May 2016. Web. August 2016.

"9 Brides Reveal Their Biggest Wedding-Day Fear." *Brides*. 15 October
	2014. Web. October 2016.

"10 things to Include in your Wedding Website." *Knotsvilla.com*. Web.